Is it so you don't

get lost at night?

Does it get brighter when you are happy?

Or dimmer when you are sad?

Does it get RED when you are feeling shy?

Or flicker
when you get mad?

And what do you do during the day?
Do you sleep, so at night you can play?

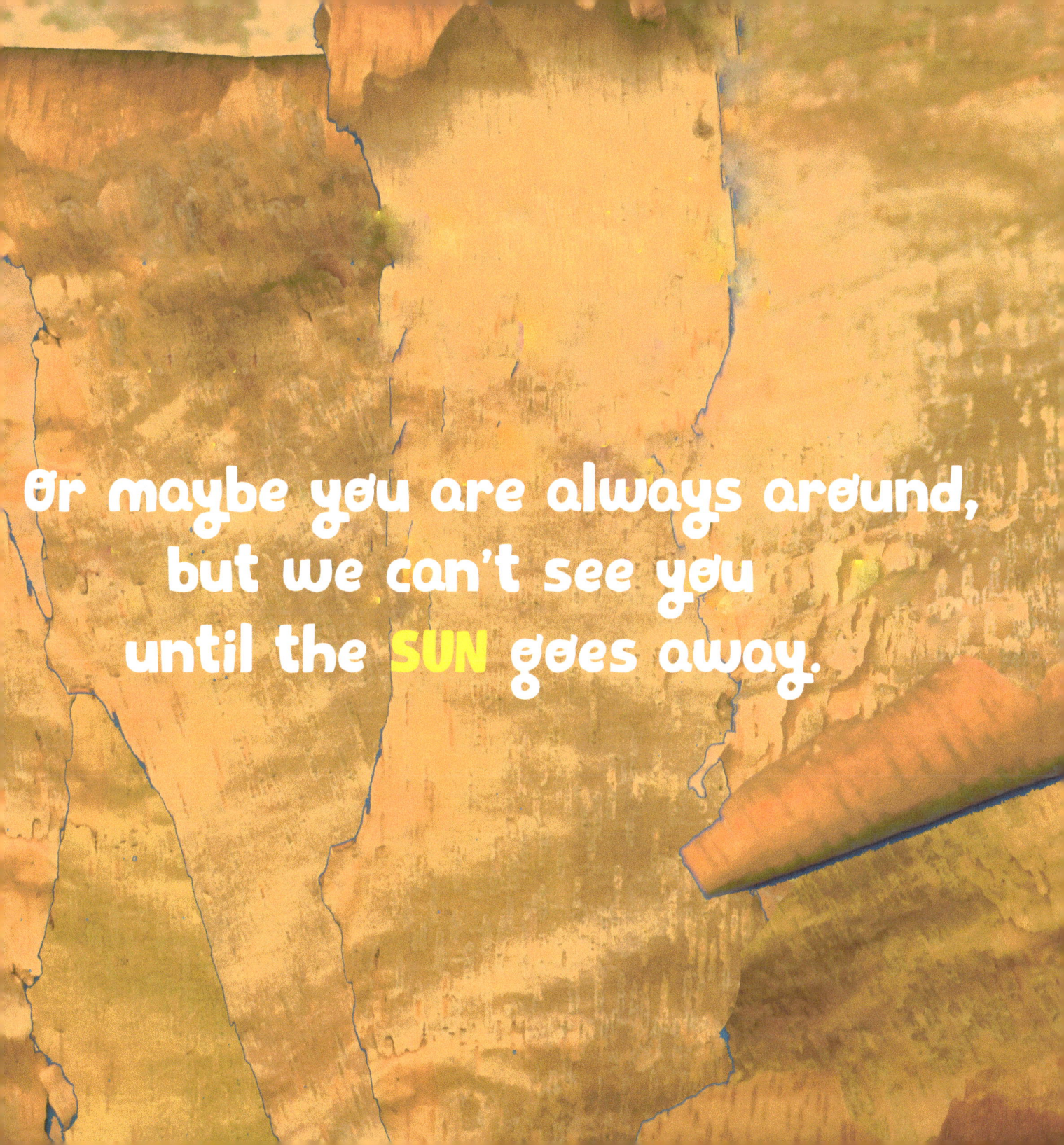

Firefly, you're a mystery, an exciting wonder of life!

But sometimes
I do feel a little sad
that we can only play at night.

Firefly facts

Fireflies talk to each other with light that flashes from their tails.
They use it mostly to talk to their friends, but they also use it to defend their home and distract predators.
The chemicals in the fireflies tail is what creates their fantastic light show!

jdanninibooks.com